HELICOPTERS

FLYING MACHINES

Kelly Baysura

Rourke Publishing LLC
Vero Beach, Florida 32964

About The Author:

Kelly Baysura graduated from Duquesne University in Pittsburgh, PA with a degree in Elementary Education. Kelly has taught grades K, 1, 4, and 5 and was most recently employed in the education field as a reading specialist.

PHOTO CREDITS:
© Jay Selman-Avion Photos: Cover, pages 1, 4, 8, 10, 12,13, 15, 18, 21
© Kelly Baysura: Pages 7, 17

EDITORIAL SERVICES:
Pamela Schroeder

Library of Congress Cataloging-in-Publication Data

Baysura, Kelly, 1970–
    Helicopters / Kelly Baysura.
        p. cm. — (Flying machines)
    Includes bibliographical references and index.
    ISBN 1-58952-004-1
    1. Helicopters—Juvenile literature. [1. Helicopters.] I. Title

TL716.2 .B39 2001
629.133'352—dc21

                                                        00-066531

Printed in the USA

TABLE OF CONTENTS

THE FIRST HELICOPTERS

People have had ideas about **helicopters** for a long time. The ancient Chinese played with a toy that looked like a helicopter. Leonardo da Vinci was an Italian inventor and artist. He made drawings of helicopters in 1480. These first helicopters were not able to fly. In 1907 Paul Cornu made the first helicopter that could fly.

Helicopters come in all shapes and sizes. This helicopter is able to seat only two people.

HOW WE USE HELICOPTERS

Helicopters are very important. Glance up at the sky. You will probably see a helicopter. Helicopters are used to carry people. They also help people who are sick or hurt get to the hospital quickly. Some helicopters are used to help fight forest fires. The police use helicopters to find criminals. Helicopters are able to do many jobs.

Helicopters are used to get people who are sick or hurt to the hospital quickly.

AMAZING ABILITIES

Helicopters are **flexible**. They can fly almost anywhere. Helicopters have abilities that airplanes do not have. Helicopters can fly forward. They can fly backward. Helicopters can fly straight up or straight down. They can even **hover** in the air. Helicopters can land on small, flat spaces. They don't need room for a runway.

The United States Navy uses helicopters. They are able to take off and land on Navy ships.

9

HOW DO HELICOPTERS FLY?

Helicopters are often called choppers because they make a loud chopping sound. The chopping noise comes from the long blades on top of the helicopter. These blades are called **rotors**. Each rotor is a spinning wing. They create **lift**—just as airplane wings do. Lift makes the helicopter fly. A helicopter has rotors on its top and on its tail.

Helicopters are sometimes used to take people to work.

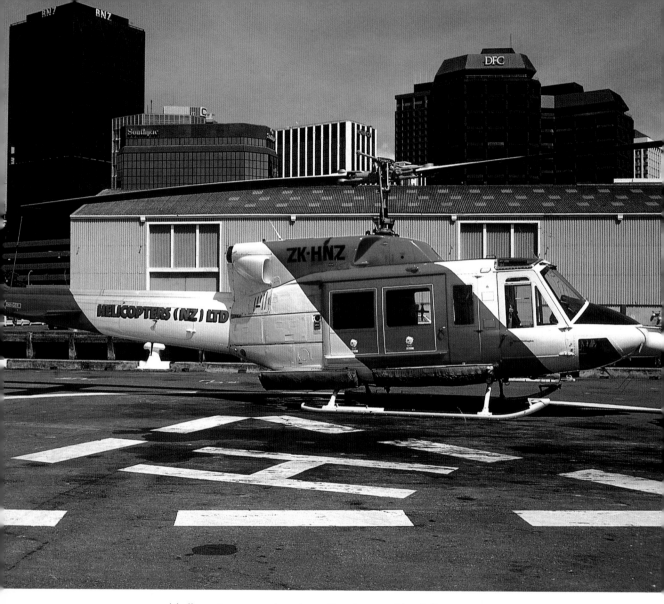

Helicopters can land on the tops of buildings.

This helicopter, a Bell 227, has two rotor blades.

The main rotor is an important part of the helicopter. The rotor blades are long, thin wings. The engine spins them around through the air. When the rotor spins, it makes lift. Lift is what allows the helicopter to fly. It also allows the helicopter to hover, turn, and change **altitude**.

The United States Marines use many types of helicopters.

WHERE DO HELICOPTERS LAND?

Landing a helicopter takes a lot of training. Pilots spend a lot of time learning how to take off and land a helicopter. Helicopters can land where planes can't. A helicopter can land on top of a building or on a road. Some helicopters have skids for landing on the ground, some have wheels and tires.

This helicopter lands using metal skids.

MILITARY HELICOPTERS

The **armed forces** use helicopters. They use them for moving troops and watching things. They also use them for moving people away from danger. Helicopters became well liked during World War II. They were used to spy on the enemy. These early helicopters did not have weapons. The early helicopter pilots were always in danger.

This Boeing helicopter carries United States Marines to remote areas.

19

TYPES OF HELICOPTERS

Helicopters come in many sizes. Some are small with only two seats. Others are large. A large helicopter can carry 50 or more people. Helicopters fly about 60 mph (97 km/h). Some can fly over 250 mph (405 km/h).

Helicopters come in a variety of sizes, shapes, and styles.

FUTURE HELICOPTERS

Now there is a new vehicle that flies like a helicopter, but looks like an airplane. The Tiltrotor aircraft takes off like a helicopter and then flies like an airplane. Long rotors lift it straight off the ground. Then the engines tilt forward and wings provide lift for the aircraft. The Tiltrotor flies twice as fast as a regular helicopter.

GLOSSARY

altitude (AL teh tood) — height above the Earth's surface

armed forces (ARMD FORS ez) — all the military, naval, and air forces of a country

flexible (FLEX seh buhl) — can easily change to fit various conditions

helicopter (HEL eh kahp ter) — aircraft without wings that is lifted from the ground and kept in the air by rotors

hover (HUV er) — stay in or near one place in the air

lift (LIFT) — to raise into the air

rotors (RO terz) — system of rotating blades by which a helicopter is able to fly

INDEX

FURTHER READING

Find out more about helicopters with these helpful books and information sites:
• www.letsfindout.com/aviation   • www.howstuffworks.com/helicopter
• www.copters.com   • www.helis.com

Berliner, Don, *Aviation: Reaching For the Sky.* The Oliver Press, Inc. 1995.,
Jennings, Terry. *Planes, Gliders, Helicopters, and Other Flying Machines.* Kingfisher Books, 1993.
Stille, Darlene. *Helicopters.* Children's Press, 1997.